From
FEAR
to
GRATITUDE

Affirmations to Build a Positive Future and
Eliminate Those Negative Thoughts

GLENN COSSAR

BALBOA.PRESS
A DIVISION OF HAY HOUSE

Balboa Press books may be ordered through booksellers or by contacting:

Balboa Press
A Division of Hay House
1663 Liberty Drive
Bloomington, IN 47403
www.balboapress.com.au
1 (877) 407-4847

Print information available on the last page.

ISBN: 978-1-5043-1946-1 (sc)
ISBN: 978-1-5043-1947-8 (e)

Balboa Press rev. date: 10/21/2019

PREFACE

I n my first book, "Yes. I Can Handle Three Things For Now." R#01 I talk about the benefits we can all gain from the use of affirmations in our lives. At the time I mentioned several examples that I have used to alleviate my own fears, doubts and troubled times.

Upon reflection, I then thought about the various times when I was not in trouble but still needed to focus my energies and thoughts and I recognised that I was doing quite a lot of self-talk to maintain my momentum.

For me the affirmation is a statement that can focus this self-talk, in a way unlike any other piece of advice or support. In fact, I have found that success requires a combination of both support and self-confidence.

We Talk all the Time

Humans have the unique ability to master speech. Wait is this right? Don't other animals also use sound and have created complex noises to indicate anger and rage as with an adult lion or bear when hunting or protecting their young. Then in a similar way birds have songs for what seems like every occasion and in fact use elegant and wonderous tones? So too do dolphins communicate in complex clicks and whistles no less clear and precise as we humans communicate?

So, to say our language is superior is simply not true, but it is different. Agreed?

Then we have the suggestions of most leading communications experts, that the "spoken" word constitutes only a tiny fraction of any messages we communicate to each other and that the vast majority is broadcast through body language and posturing and then tone and inflection of our voices. We are all familiar with people who say things like; "I just have to get through this" but their body language is far from positive, as is their tone of voice. This body language reveals their failed attempts at masking their pain to the extent that even they do not believe what they are staying.

Now we all know these contradictions to be true, and we all have similar examples, such as the reluctant apology where the words are "I am VERY sorry!" said through clenched teeth and in the angriest most defiant voice possible! We instinctively recognise the lie for exactly what it is, before that short phrase is even completed.

What is happening here is that words are important in communication but what is more important is the "delivery" of those words. Successful communication includes our posture and our tone, to make the message believable.

From a very early age all creatures great and small including humans who will recognise a lie when it is spoken by watching for the visual cues and resonating sounds being projected. I say this is important because when using affirmations to boost or change how we feel we first must change our posture and delivery tone to make our communications to ourselves meaningful and believable.

Our most influential audience when communicating is ourselves.

After all, ... **we talk all the time** ... and the single most attentive audience is **us**!

The ability to use our self-talk or positive thinking as a means of boosting our senses and in particular our self-confidence is well supported from many successful therapists and writers spanning centuries.

I use these affirmations as *negativity busters* that really work!

Any search of a local library and the internet will also present plenty of books, articles and discussions about how our self-talk can make a difference to how we feel and how we deal with life's challenges, and I contend we can shift into a more accepting and positive position by focusing on the way we self-talk.

"I wake up today with strength in my heart and clarity in my mind." Dr. Carmen Harra. R#02

In these pages I offer an extended look at affirmations and how, by using them well, we can all make a big difference in helping ourselves be more positive, more in control and more able to focus to create a life that is full of amazing adventures.

I have included the samples written previously in my earlier look at affirmations from my book "Three Things" and then I have expanded and added to them.

Grouped to Suit Your Situation

I have also made my best effort to group them or classify them, to fit into some situations and circumstances that most of us experience at any time.

I hope this helps you to identify the right affirmation for the right situation.

Whilst I have created this set of affirmations to cover most situations, I acknowledge they may not be for everyone. These are amongst my best attempts but they really only scratch the surface of what would be regarded as a complete list. You may well have others and I certainly encourage you to keep using the ones that resonate best for you.

Perhaps even write down some of your own and keep them close by. I have included a space at the back of this book for you to do this.

Accordingly, I set down the challenge for you, to follow up and offer your own affirmations and to share with me those you cherish and find useful. I am grateful if you do send me what works for you or those people close to you. I may be able to include them in any future editions. So please don't hold back.

Cautiously, I also mention that being positive alone, never replaces clear and decisive action to make things happen.

I always suggest that people plan to do at least *'three things'* each day and to do so with a very determined attitude.

This can be where the use of positive thinking or affirmations can really help to focus your thoughts. I feel they add to that positive and determined attitude and in turn add to your success. You may even have an experience filled with joy and wonder at our own ability to get things done and you can celebrate these thoughts with an appropriate affirmation. See chapter #6 Gratitude, for more ideas.

I truly hope you enjoy reading what I offer and that you are able to make use of any words and phrases that help you find your way in this amazing world we share.

Best wishes for a great future, filled with confidence, creativity and compassion.

Glenn Cossar

DEDICATION:

For my two amazing daughters Melanie May and Elise Klarenbeek and their life partners and husbands Martin May, and Owen Klarenbeek. These two men not only share their wives' experiences but also offer unconditional love and support to them with great generosity, particularly when things can get a bit tough.

Also, to all those seeking a better now and a better future no matter what may lay ahead.

I accept that life is all at once;
good, bad and indifferent.
and I choose to celebrate that
which brings
joy and love to all.

Glenn ©

CONTENTS

CHAPTER 1

OVERCOMING FEAR

There is much written and talked about regarding fear and its power over us and also our use of it to force others to do what we want. I cannot adequately cover all aspects of fear and its various forms in this one book. In this context of self-talk and affirming our own support, the negative aspects of fear can be to reduce or eliminate the positive steps we take on things like our vulnerability, accepting risks, and presenting our public face to the world.

Let me say early on, that I believe it to be unfair to say to people, "Be strong" or, "Move on" or, "Just get over it and make it work." When we are fragile and in need of support these statements or advice tend to remind us that we are *not* being strong, or *not* able to move forward, nor that we may be capable of making anything positive happen.

Then it is almost cruel to tell people to do something they clearly cannot do at this point in time.

My affirmations try to acknowledge the struggle and offer some reminder to the user that we are all capable to do something, even if that something is just reciting an affirmation.

Just this simple act of stating a wish for better times is enough until we can make a start on what we know we need to do.

As for fear, it has an impact on us all because many people have used it to their advantage over the course of human history. People use it still today, and I have no doubt will continue to use it far into the future.

We see people use fear to drive others to achieve, regardless of the hate and pain it also creates. Coaches who yell at us, that bad boss who threatens to dock us pay or-worse-to sack us, even parents have used threats and coercion to get results at times.

You know something? It does work, but only for a limited time and then the emotional pain starts to settle in and people resent the disrespect it represents or ask, "Why is it necessary to insult me to keep me motivated?" or "There has to be a better way, surely?"

Whatever gain is made from making others afraid or by threatening to take away what we have, we remain in that constant fear of grief and loss when fear is used against us.

There *is* a better way!

I am suggesting that the use of affirmations can be that part of our set of tools or resources that provide this better way.

"I will face my fear. I will permit it to pass over and through me. And when it is gone past, I will turn the inner eye to see its path. Where the fear has gone there will be nothing. Only I will remain." (Frank Herbert-*Dune*) R#03

This use of fear never goes well for a long-term successful and supportive life. If this is true, how then do we face fear when it is presented to us? How can we be strong and relentless when we are so afraid?

The following affirmations are offered as a means to arrive at a place of peace, capable and ready to act. Just as a sailing ship seeks a port of calm away from those storming seas, before returning to its journey, we too often need to re-focus before returning to our action plans.

These affirmations allow our ship-of-hope to continue sailing towards our better future, free from the crippling effects of trepidation and fear.

What about My Irrational Fears?

We all have that nagging feeling that something may be upset if we change our routine or what I like to call our "pattern of success". This anxiety and self-imposed stress do not seem like something we do to ourselves, but often they are. Superstitions are made from this need to replicate what went well, even if we have no logical connection to the actions or feelings and the previous success.

We may even add compulsive steps like rattling a locked doorknob or checking three times that the car is locked before we trust that it is in fact safe before we walk around it four times and finally go shopping. Funny eh?

No, this is us adding fear of some loss to our actions and giving rise to abject superstitious behavior. We mistakenly believe, the fear of loss can be overcome with bizarre actions and rituals. I am not referring to forms of illness that cause obsessive behaviors. I am not qualified to comment on those. I am referring to similar behaviors that crop up from time to time when life is a bit overwhelming.

This feeling of being overwhelmed can affect all of us and so we do what is helpful to get by even if it means we adopt a bizarre ritual of knocking on wood or sitting in the exact same seat wherever we go least our good fortune be tempted to abandon us.

The best way to reduce or eliminate this fear is to observe the "facts" and rely on them.

If you are missing some elements of fact, please don't invent superstitious beliefs, in place of these essential relevant facts needed to make decisions and to even act in everyday situations.

Tom would say to me "But Glenn, what if she thinks I am an idiot and leaves me, because I did not get that promotion?" I reply, "Tom, are you having an unfounded belief or are you willing to ask your new wife about how she feels regarding your promotional prospects? Can you get the real facts, before you start to worry?"

Tom blinks at me and says, "But what if I ask her and she leaves me because I asked?" I make sure I do not trivialize how he feels because this is serious to Tom and he clearly is asking for help. I suggest that he weigh up the consequences of asking or not asking and that he again rely on the facts and not rely on unsubstantiated thoughts or beliefs.

Fear and the fear of the unknown are real life killers, but it does exist within us to protect us from very practical incidents of danger, not the imaginary or superstitious belief about how the universe really works. I will talk more about how fear helps us as a survival tool a little further on.

The caterpillar: *"As a caterpillar, I used to fear becoming something else, something unknown and I felt so unprepared."*

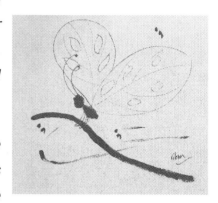

The butterfly: *"I realise now everything I was doing was preparing me for an amazing future. A future I now adore."*

Here are some of my affirmations that I offer to help when dealing with fear and all that it does to hold us back:

1. Hello, fear. You have come to hold me back again, but shall we walk this way and that, along your well-worn track? So, I can show you I am not ever going back.

2. My confidence and courage does not stop me feeling afraid, but they do remind me of how I can carry on to face yet another day.

3. I am calm, I am confident, I am prepared. These truths I know are enough to help me face my fears and to overcome them.

Fear is a Useful Survival Tool

Now don't get me wrong. As an effective internal alarm, fear works great to keep us alive. This is especially true when we are contemplating a walk over that highway full of big body-busting trucks and we stop by the curb and think, *Nah ... I will probably get hit, better to go back inside that bar and finish my drink. Maybe, I will get a taxi home .... Yeah, I will do that.* Fear works a treat in this instance to stop us becoming roadkill.

However, when we start looking hard for things that scare our pants off and it becomes an obsession that cripples us from achieving our hopes and dreams, then we have a problem.

Nerada, said to me once, "Glenn, I am so scared of people laughing at me, I actually vomit every time I am about to go on stage. *Ohhhh* I will never be good enough. What do you think I should do?" Nerada is a beautiful ballet dancer with many years of stage experience, and yes she is still learning her craft but I remind her, "Nerada, it matters little what I think or anyone else thinks for that matter. You have the training, the skill, and the passion for your art. People light up every time you set foot on that stage. As soon as they see your wonderful smile and the poise and grace of your obviously practiced performance, I see them rise in their seats so they don't miss a single moment."

Nerada knows she can dance and hold the attention of a full auditorium, and like all of us she has moments of self-doubt, and this can become a real fear of not doing her best. For Nerada, a short reminder of her true potential is all that is needed to bust those negative thoughts.

For people who have a recent history of pain and disappointment, more may be needed. For those who have a deeper past of betrayal or trauma, a lot more support is required.

There are some in our communities who have experienced terrible histories, even terrible generational pain. This is something fear clings to and robs people of their dignity, strangles their health, and empties their heart. This sounds bad and it is bad, but surprisingly, or perhaps not surprisingly, these same people can not only cope with such trauma but thrive from their individual determination for success.

This strength and determination is not an earned thing nor is it something we can gain; it is inherently part of us always and forever.

Please read this last sentence again. This personal strength, I believe has always been within us all, no matter the depth of pain, no matter how lost someone may feel at a particular time.

Our inner strength is resilient and lies deep within us. However, it must be awakened and remembered!

A path to remembering involves; determination, and above all a self-belief that knows no boundaries. With the help of some targeted self-talk it rises high above our challenges, and take us to places and situations we may not even imagine are possible.

Let's take a look at a few places where this self-talk can help us remember our inner strength:

4. For all those who rely on me; my children, my colleagues, myself, I am most definitely the best that I can be, when I believe in myself.

5. I know my knees may knock and my stomach turn, but when I face my fear, I also know this fear I feel today, through my use of determination, shall not return anytime soon.

6. I alone determine that my body shall stop its rush and accept that it needs to rest. I call on my inner strength and stand tall, no matter what may come.

7. Yesterday I was calm and I will be calm again today and whenever again I may need to be. It is I who decides this.

8. Critics will always come and go. However, I will endure, and my future is what I choose to do for myself and for those I love and care for.

9. I am never diminished by what others say or do. Their lives are their own just as my life is mine. A life which is as amazing as I choose it to be.

Fear is Not Always Obvious

With those last few affirmations, I am trying to show that fear is not always obvious and can sneak up on us in everyday situations such as when we may doubt ourselves. More about doubt later.

We often worry that we are not good enough or have too much to lose to take a chance on life. This is particularly true when we have faced failure way too many times in the past, or when we are facing criticism, again and again and feel we are diminished by others and what they think or say about us. Our self-talk is very powerful because we believe its truth despite knowing we have much to offer that is good.

So then, if we can talk ourselves into submission, so too can we talk ourselves into a more powerful and positive version of ourselves. Perhaps even powerful enough to deal with challenges thrown our way, and maybe, just maybe, powerful enough to smash that shit into another universe and stand tall again to make today the best day ever!

Let's look at some more fear busting affirmations:

10. I am open and trusting of others who can help me achieve my greatest hopes, dreams and goals.

11. My pain, and my fear of further pain is unbearable. So, I choose to disregard it and walk amongst my demons, first passing one then another and yet another. All are in awe of my courage which is simply me walking with my fear firmly in my grip, least it escapes to taunt me.

12. I am alone and frightened, frightened and alone. And yet I stand to face another day. Another day I stand and still I do not fall.

Acceptance of Negativity and Positivity as a Normal Part of Life

We all know that feeling of dread, when negativity puts us in a grip of panic and we feel helplessly overwhelmed.

Maybe not all of us, all of the time, but this is a frequent occurrence for some of us and it can be very debilitating. This can be the same feeling we feel when we are standing tall at the highest diving board, or looking over the edge of a skyscraper or cliff lookout.

The latter experience can be both exhilarating or can induce a sense of panic should we have to jump!

For some the act of bungee-jumping off a bridge offers this excitement, for others the thrill of a roller-coaster does the same thing.

However, if this physiological change is happening when we anticipate a phone call to our boss at work, or a conversation with our spouse or partner, then something else is happening and it is usually "fear".

This feeling of dread gives power to those negative thoughts and before you know it, fear has taken hold and sent chemicals racing through our bodies at a pace we must respond to. The likely responses are the three fs-flight, fight or freeze!

Our brain stem has a core response operating to initiate survival for us and within a split second, one of these three will be chosen.

In order for us to respond physically, our brain sends signals to produce adrenalin so that our muscles can act and produce a gold medal quality sprint. This increased physical capability is so that we can flee from whatever danger is about to destroy us. Similarly, should fighting be necessary, our strength is momentarily upskilled to deal with the attack. Also, our capacity to stand incredibly still and blend into our environment requires a great deal of physical strength.

Without this release of tension built up to handle a physical response, in the case of that phone call to the scary boss, we are left with a feeling of overwhelming stress and possibly anxiety.

As a survival technique, this rising feeling of panic and fear helps to keep us alive in dangerous situations and so we learn to value the way it works.

So then, what is possibly given less value, than fear induced super powers, is our capacity to discover positive and safe options or situations that offer love, peace and joy.

These warm and inviting feelings are often seen to be of no use in an emergency. But the irony is that by loving ourselves and others we are more capable of exploring options to the emergency in a calm and measured way that does not generate stress and anxiety.

Instead of hiding or ignoring our capacity for love, we can mitigate this and provide a solution to any aberrant negativity by adopting a more positive approach to life. Literally, we can build a capability to look on the bright side of any situation.

This takes both, time and courage.

Often you will hear people say something similar to this, "Paul, just count to ten before you start swinging punches, OK?" or you may have heard others say, "Just breath for a few seconds and calm yourself before you jump to any conclusions."

As with my friend Paul, his quick temper and ability to punch away at street gangs was a real advantage whilst we were teens growing up in a very rough neighborhood. However, this skill did not sit well with his new wife and kids. He asked me, "Glenn, how can I make the change from street warrior to gentle dad. I just get angry when the kids talk back to me. I am not used to this softly-softly approach. What am I supposed to do mate? I just feel like I am making things worse and they would be better off without me!"

Fear and self-doubt are a cruel inhibitor, but it is also a deadly killer when a person believes that they are useless, never likely to amount to something and eventually start to think they have no right to be alive.

Suicide is a silent killer because it is not spoken about nor is it addressed well enough yet to prevent the numbers of people in our community we currently lose.

At times fear and doubt can reach a stage where anyone can say to themselves that their loved ones would be better off without them.

The answer to this horror situation is of course more complex than just reciting a few affirmations. Paul and I did talk about changing expectations and applying Paul's obvious strengths in a different direction. Among other helpful strategies, he decided to adopt some specific affirmations that dealt with his fear of not being in control as well as his doubts of being a great dad.

Paul is now managing his temper better since he understood that his expectations were holding him back. He is now more relaxed about his responsibilities and he is enjoying being "in the moment" with his children and they also have noticed this positive difference.

These doubts can be as equally crippling as fear, so let's explore doubt in my next chapter.

CHAPTER 2

IN TIMES OF DOUBT

At times we all feel a little inadequate whilst life demands that we be confident and strong against challenges and the things that are really hard, or seemingly impossible.

The reality for many of us, is that we don't feel strong and confident all the time and that some challenges are just too hard for us to handle.

In these moments we need something more than another person telling us to, "Come on – just be strong", particularly when we feel we can't go on, or we just don't know what to do next.

"You are interesting, layered, comforting and fun because of your imperfections, not despite them. Being imperfect is, without doubt, a very good thing." *Kate James. R#04.*

The following affirmations are suggested to be used in a moment of quiet contemplation to remind us of *how* we can proceed and then how we can make a difference. That difference, or change for the better, is exactly what we need to access. In these times when we doubt our capability and when we may even doubt ourselves, a reminder of our capability really helps.

Here are some affirmations for when doubt stops you in your tracks:

1. I am a force to be reckoned with and nothing will stop me achieving my hopes, my dreams, and my goals.

2. This time things are different and I know this. I am prepared, I am capable. I will succeed.

3. I am a good person, I do good things, and I can make a difference.

We are all "Good People"

This last one about being a good person, literally was my personal affirmation for many years when life presented me with too many challenges. At that time, I thought I could not cope and, in those days, I barely made it out of bed in the morning let alone feel brave enough, strong enough, smart enough to face the day!

Through tears I would begin by looking in my morning mirror and to say these words over and over again until I could take that long breath and tell myself, "This feeling will pass … I don't know when or how, but it will pass. ……
It must pass. Please let it pass today."

And so, another day would begin with a slow stagger out the front door and into my world of loneliness and pain. Now, I was not completely alone, I had my two wonderful daughters and close friends who were wishing me well. But I was experiencing that level of being alone in a crowded room and no-one, not even those close to me could understand what I was facing and how I was assembling my best self to overcome my personal challenges of being alone without a life partner or the prospect of starting my life all over again.

I literally needed to do this every day and at times even during the day, especially when those feelings of self-doubt would arise unexpectedly.

Overcome them I did, and this single affirmation became my go-to phrase and has become the trigger to ignite my inner strength to this day.

I also think, because they are my own words, it has power and value to me personally.

So then, I recommend that if you are able to muster a few words that resonate with yourself and your own situation, they will serve you far better than anything I write here. Perhaps my affirmations can inspire you to create your own go-to or power phrase! You can use the spare pages at the back of this book to record your own affirmations.

Please let me know when you do. I would love to hear about how it works for you.

Here are some more doubt busters to get you thinking:

4. Today has brought me an opportunity to grow as a person and I know that my knowledge, my skills, and my belief in myself are more than enough to meet this challenge.

5. Yesterday was hard, today just got worse. Tomorrow may be better or it may not. I shall hope for a day that will inspire me to look forward with joy and kindness in my heart.

6. I am prepared, strong, and determined to get things done.

7. Today, tomorrow, and forever, I am both worthy and proud to be the very best that I am.

8. My body has just reminded my mind that I have something I want to do today.

9. Today, I am capable, clever, and ready for anything.

10. I am able to add a positive influence through engagement with others. Together, with other people by my side, I find that I can accept pain a little easier and I can also offer support to those in need.

11. I shall be kind and never rude, creative and never judgmental, loving and never fueled by hate.

12. Is this who I am? YES. Is this where I am meant to be? YES. Is this all there is? NO … I have much to do and when it is begun and finally done, my happy celebration will be so much fun.

We all, Each of us Have so Much to Offer

Just as #12 states, we "have much to do" and so much more to offer. This remains true no matter how much we may doubt our skills and abilities. Other people may be better at things that we think we could be good at, and that is fine.

That is fine for them, but for us, we too have a capacity to reach out for our true potential. Finding that true potential can be challenging. It is also a lot of fun when we approach it with a positive outlook.

What do I mean by saying the words, "True Potential"? You may ask, "Surely potential is something we can aim for and expect our efforts to reach at any time?"

My answer, "No!" I feel we cannot truly see our potential. It is as if we have a veil over any premonition of our future that stops us from forecasting what we can actually do or become, despite us imagining what it may be like.

I have an idea why this is so. I see it as true from my personal experience, and also from witnessing those close to me, that so many people achieve their success, and that they could not even imagine achieving it as a prediction. Similarly, not all negative events can be foretold.

Again, why is this so? I believe it is because, to anticipate a very specific outcome would inhibit ourselves searching for the *optimum* results within an ever-changing environment, that is our reality.

For example, if I were to plough a field and wait for rain before planting a crop and it never comes, how am I to know the right time to plant? I can rely on past history and a good deal of charting the previous seasons, but I can never accurately predict a damaging flood, nor a crippling injury to myself that prevents me from planting at that exact time. Or, for that matter I cannot foresee a fortunate turn of events that brings me extra friends or people to work on my farm one year, enabling me to have a bumper crop and enough seed for the next three years.

Nature offers the randomness of our worldly events.

We must adapt to take advantage of the changes in order to optimise results. We simply must gather what information we can and then give it our best effort.

Without prior knowledge of exactly what may happen I can only *do-my-best* and assemble enough resources to make it work at that exact point in time!

My potential to be successful then, relies partly on events beyond my anticipation or even my comprehension, and partly on my preparation.

I do have this potential regardless of any situation though, and I can create a robust opportunity for it to happen with my preparation and optimism. I keep watching for those many opportunities to come my way. Like a comet hurtling through the cosmos, good fortune is there for the taking by those brave enough and ready enough to grab at it.

The latter represents me being positive in my thinking, so that I am ready to act when good opportunities do pass my way.

Rest assured negative opportunities will also pass me by and I also need to watch out and avoid them as best I can. In particular those doubts that scream inside my head, "I just can't afford to fail again." These negativities are so seductive and sound so rational at the time, because the weight of negativity is strong, but always they must be challenged so that some perspective can arise and be equally heard.

I feel that a focus on activity and past achievements can assist in gaining that positive outlook and our self-talk takes that central role of leading our thoughts to positivity and future actions.

This can endorse our action planning and provide a path to small and then larger successful outcomes.

I believe that the use of affirmations can keep my mind clear of negativity and focused on identifying those positives at all times as a means to my success.

I have mentioned several times the concept of challenges, what I mean by this are those events and situations that stop us or appear to present confusion and doubt as well as choices to take. Even a choice between two good things can be a challenge. These choices can and do, cause us to procrastinate, so in this next chapter, I explore the art of busting procrastination.

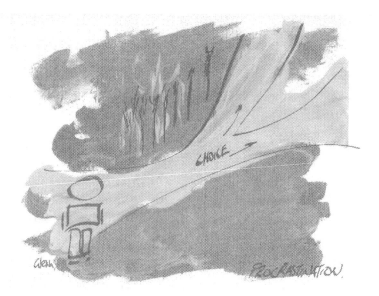

CHAPTER 3

DEALING WITH PROCRASTINATION

B eing a willing participant to delay, means accepting actions that send you off-track to another place that is not the one where you wanted to be.

How often have we all suddenly asked ourselves "Where am I?" or "What was I supposed to be doing?" This is because we are allowing procrastination to take centre stage instead of a focus of what we want. Often our progress relies on making and taking choices, not always between just one or the other, but many choices to start things we want to progress.

It is so easy to be caught up in the decision-making process that we lose sight of the fact we have chosen already to make that start.

Risk is all around us and we are likely to make a bad choice sometimes, but usually this is nothing that can't be either undone or fixed by yet another choice. Unless of course it is a life and death decision, hopefully these are rare and we do need to make these with all the facts and consequences well thought out. Even then a final choice must be made and made with confidence whilst putting aside any fears and regrets.

Procrastination, rarely offers a place of contentment. It is also often wrapped in nice things like; sleep, food, entertainment, time with friends or family, multiple chores around the house that always need doing.

These chores or tasks include washing clothes and cleaning and sorting and even organising the sock drawer or the cutlery into its various sub-categories of existence. All seemingly productive tasks, but they are not the tasks that are a priority, nor are they the tasks we really need or want to perform …. RIGHT NOW!!!

So, what is it that is stopping you doing those important things you want and need to do? Is it a fear of failure, if so, you must quickly jump to chapter #1 and check out that fear? It may be that we are just too tired, but beware this is another deceptive wrapping to avoid.

Is it a lack of preparation that is holding you back? Then make a list of what you need to do, or have to do, that will get things started. An important element to getting things started and done is our self-belief.

These affirmations may help you on your way. Maybe attempt two or three;

1. Despite feeling low and unsure, I actually am ready, and I am prepared. I can and will start right now.

2. Today is the day, the best day. Today is the day I shall begin.

3. I have reached my fork in the road. The path before me is clear and as tempting as it may be, I shall not look back, because to do that will use up the time I have chosen to continue on my path.

How Does Self-Care Impact on our Ability to be Ready?

Often, we have neglected our own capacity to work and or even rest and play, by not attending to our physical and mental health.

This ability to self-care is essential to a happy productive life. There are many reasons why we don't take care of ourselves and this can be because we see others as needing our care and attention more than ourselves. Also, we may see value in making time for others and feel selfish if we schedule that long warm shower or an afternoon at the movies or that day off once in a while. In many cultures self-sacrifice is regarded as a virtue. I feel this obsession with self-sacrifice is incorrect and not a good thing to be proud of.

That old saying, "Keep your cup full so that you may tip some kindness or love into someone's empty cup." is more important to bear in mind when we are preparing for some tough or challenging times ourselves.

An empty cup has nothing to give. This is true for when we are giving our energy to help others but even more so, when it is us who need that extra amount of energy to overcome our procrastination.

A key element in making progress is recognising that we too need preparation and support to make a leap into the unknown or to tackle some hard work that is headed our way. By making sure we are the focus of some rejuvenation or simply a good time, can allow us to bust any delay tactics we may put in our way and we feel so much more ready to make good things happen.

The act of self-sabotage is real and is also an extreme form of procrastination. Guarding against this is achieved by being aware we are doing it in the first place, but also by reflecting on when it happens so we can guard against it in the future.

My good friend Jim would say, "Glenn, it doesn't matter what I am doing, as soon as I decide to knuckle down and do some study, some disaster is found by the family to derail me! I can't seem to get a break these days. Maybe, part-time study and family just doesn't mix eh?"

Now Jim, has great intentions, but he is not aware that these *disasters* are largely his own inventions.

Yes, he must place a priority on his family, but at some point, his study is also a priority that is deserving of rising to the top. The family can either hold off or better yet, be empowered to attempt attending to whatever they are able to do and allow Jim to progress his hopes and dreams.

Similarly, for Jim to be truly *response-able* (responsible) he must be fit and capable to respond to whatever is in his focus of attention right now. When Jim is working from a place of physical or emotional exhaustion, he is not at his best and an optimum outcome is not going to eventuate.

This setting of his own priorities is largely within Jim's responsibility and can be assisted with some focus on his part through the strategic use of affirmations.

Here are a couple I would recommend for Jim:

4. Today I begin working on my life goals, because they are important to me.

5. No one else but me is responsible for me. I can do what I need to do and what I want to do, and when I want to do it.

6. My happiness and success is within me and not external. No one else, no place nor thing holds my potential for success but me.

Self-confidence Can be so Elusive

"Just be confident Glenn, and the world will fall at your feet." She said. This was a strong phrase from an older mentor, but not one that resonated with me at a time when I was feeling very vulnerable, depressed and lost without a job and wondering how I would feed my family and pay the bills. It certainly did not inspire me to achieve great things or get my mojo back!

She was right though about my confidence. It had suffered badly from recent events and this was showing, but the way for me to regain it was to be a much slower process than how quickly it was lost.

My confidence and self-belief had been a wavering thing during adolescence but was strongest in early childhood and stronger again when I was in my thirties and established in my career. The difference was that I noticed people around me shared my self-belief at these times. Early on my mother had shown me unconditional love and support, together with respectful feedback when I needed correction (sometimes often, I can be a slow learner at times).

So then if we have support when we feel fragile, this can buffer those negative thoughts. But the most obvious confidence builder for me was taking action, any action, no matter how small or insignificant it may appear, and completing those tasks with care and attention and then realising I had done that, I then felt satisfied with my efforts.

What happens once we have something to look back on that we are happy with or even proud of, is that other people notice. That care and attention exercised to complete these tasks genuinely, are attractive to others who then offer support and want to be part of the success we generate. This process builds self-confidence around our past success. It may also be the strongest type of self-care we practice. I believe it also contributes to that phenomenon I refer to as abundance.

The small stuff of, preparing a nice meal, staying neat and tidy, being kind to others, working hard on a task for others and attending to the necessary detail, following instructions and keeping to time as requested, placing a focus on quality, are things we can take pride in. These actions build confidence over time because we can look back at such recent events and validate to ourselves that we do matter and can make a difference not only in other people's lives but also our own.

Here are a couple of affirmations that may assist in building that self-confidence we can all use to get things going:

7. Hello world, welcome to what I can show you. Let me share my effort so that I may practice for my future success.

8. I am confident that my skills and preparation are more than enough to do what I need to do.

9. Now is the right time, now is the best time, NOW is MY time.

I Can't See it Yet

What we can't see, is not necessarily hidden, it may just be slightly out of sight.

We have all played the game of peek-a-boo either as children or with young children. The excitement and laughter that comes with it is infectious and wonderful. It is also a bit scary for some.

I recently played peek-a-boo with my two-year-old grandson and whilst he knew I was just around the corner, he was enjoying the surprise appearance and wanted more. But as soon as I started playing too well, by hiding where he could not easily find me and developing the game into hide-and-seek, the sense of excitement had clearly led to some stress and he wanted the game to return to the more obvious peek-a-boo format.

For a moment the game got a bit scary and my grandson looked to me for assurance that I would not disappear again.

This innocent exchange leads me to remember that the unknown can be both exciting and frightening for us more grown up types. It may also account for increased procrastination as the fear quotient tends to rise when we are unaware of what our potential is.

Perhaps too many variables can lead to hidden perils that we do not want to find, and then we freeze in our plans and actions.

So, what then did my wonderful grandson teach me?

He taught me that fun and games are everywhere and that there is a fine line between a game and a real-life consequence such as fearing the unknown.

As adults we need to know the difference and also understand that whilst the unknown can be frightening it can also mean that a pleasant surprise can be just out of sight and worthy of us taking the effort, like my grandson did, to find Grandpa or for us to find that new customer, or that new love, or that pay rise, or that new business opportunity, or that improved health and happiness we are searching for.

I marvel at people who are able to see around those corners and visualise what is just out of sight as real and tangible. Then something wonderful happens when they reach for it with all the confidence of a two-year-old just about to surprise Grandpa. It is this confidence we all must find, or perhaps we must simply remember how to play peek-a-boo with life and look forward to those good times we think are hidden from us? I like to think a game of peek-a-boo helps make life fun. What do you think?

Here are some more procrastination busters for you to think about;

10. I am not perfect and I like it. I am still able to learn more this way, and I like that I can do this. I like this very much.

11. I cannot keep these possessions when I finally depart, so I shall focus on building true wealth in my character and my gifts of love to others. This is my true legacy to those who are left to continue, my material possessions are not.

12. My feet are as lead, my step is too slow to measure and here I still rise triumphant and by my own wishes I free myself clear of these weights that hold me down. I rise to take my rightful place, at work, at rest and at play.

CHAPTER 4

ACKNOWLEDGING FAILURE AS PART OF SUCCESS

F ailure is an old friend who taps me on the shoulder and says, "Come dance with me a while. I have another lesson for you Glenn."

I welcome this moment to learn and then rest and be more prepared for success that will eventually come my way.

I also feel it is important to differentiate the act of **acceptance** from applying a false **positivity.** Acceptance of our failures is much more liberating than papering over them with false positivity.

I believe it is wrong and it is too easy to say to ourselves, "This was meant to be and I will be better for it." And, "Just stay positive." Or to say, "Just stay strong." We do hear this being said in the face of failure and then to expect all that follows will proceed to success.

The truth is far from this state of self-deception. It can feel at times that the use of an affirmation will fit into this concept of positive thinking and of hoping things may change without action. The expectation that comes from using an affirmation is that, by repeating a clear statement of support or intent that success will just happen.

In my experience it does not, unless it is followed up with clear action and some hard work to make things happen.

Our circumstances can certainly change as a result of thinking positively instead of thinking negatively, but real change is only inspired by such thinking. The action taken then, is the actual catalyst for change.

So, then acceptance of a situation is the first step of creating this change that is needed.

An affirmation or a statement of intent begins this process of positive change because it gives us a focus on what that change may look like.

We cannot deny the pain or reality of the feelings of disappointment and even shame that are companions to our failure. I might add here that these very real feelings are legitimate, but the failure is often only a "temporary failure" and it is not always permanent. Big call I know, but bear with me on this.

What we can do, is to accept that something happened that we did not want to happen, and then to keep this moment as a stepping stone or a place holder for our next attempt at either our next try or to keep exploring another way to go forward.

These stepping stones or place holders offer us hope and a reminder to follow our chosen path to our end place of real success. They offer a realisation that we still need to do more.

I do hasten to add that; all this work can be very tiresome and all soooo boring. Right? So, then you may want to read my first book, "Yes. I Can Handle Three Things for Now." In *Three Things* I explore what is possible by way of completing only three strategic actions in a positive direction, then resting and even spending time to play as a way of rejuvenating or recreating our energies. With these three actions completed a positive momentum is achieved and we give ourselves inspiration from this success to then do more.

If you practice my approach to life, I assure you that more energy and more joy is the result. For me the balance of three things of; work, rest, and play, is the key to my own success.

Behind every successful juggler may well be thousands of broken plates and cups that they have dropped before mastering their art of juggling.

These breakages are indeed temporary failures of the juggler's eventual success. It is only through their practice and self-belief and by affirming success, that the juggler perfects their skill.

If that same juggler stops at the one last broken plate and never attempts the next one, they may never realise that the next one will in fact stay up and spin. That juggler who stops may never know that they are to be successful with just one more try.

This analogy does not fit all success or all failure stories but I hope you see my point.

We all fail, most of us do fail nearly every day. We also succeed almost every single day. We have initial success, then fail then succeed again. This process can be satisfying, particularly if we get to make forward progress from this level of success. But when we move on from that imperfect sandwich, we made for lunch to being dumped in a long-term relationship or suffer a job loss, this can be a painful, sad and regrettable experience. But when we look twice at that dodgy sandwich, we somehow never give it a thought again, and accept that failure can be part of success, as our next lunch preparation can be awesome. After all, it's just a sandwich – right?

Similarly, that past relationship failure does not define our very existence but it may impact on how we look at our future success, if we fear a future failure. Some determination and patience top and bottom with a filling of love and connection may bring something amazing?

Why then do the *big* failures matter more and in other times not so much? And why do the *little* failures hurt so much at other times?

Here are some affirmations I use to motivate my thoughts past such failures, but I will explore this question of *why* a bit later:

1. Each time I fail I find another quality within me that I was not aware of and this will lead me to my future success.

2. I practised yesterday, today I am better. Along the way I will fail. I will continue to practise to improve my skills.

3. I have failed before and will no doubt fail again. It is my path to real success and I walk it willingly.

What you do makes a difference, and you have to decide what kind of difference you want to make. Jane Goodall R#05

This quote from Jane Goodall, the celebrated anthropologist and nature conservationist, captures for me the sentiment of recognising how much of a difference one individual does make in the lives of many others and in some situations the history of us all.

People like Goodall, Ghandi, Mandela, Shakespeare, Galileo and so many more from within humanity's legacy have been remarkable, because they had the courage to share their thoughts and actions despite what must have been insurmountable challenges.

These challenges would have included daily failures.

We may not all have the chance to change the face of human history, but we do have the very real chance to change the course of our own history. We can and do impact in a very positive way the course or path for those we love and care deeply about.

In my third book, *"Rebuilding the Village"* I will be showcasing some extraordinary things being done by very ordinary people in my local community. From providing a safe and experiential venue for children to learn, to supporting the homeless, to gathering others in the simple act of kindness. I will be writing about people who were undeterred by fear and failure to make something wonderful happen.

Here are some more of my affirmations that may inspire you to keep going to realise those amazing goals of yours:

4. I stand, I fail, I cry, I crash, and yet here I stand again and again. If you witness me standing you witness another step I have taken toward my success.

5. I have ploughed my field, I have sown my seeds, and I have watched the rain fall to bring life to my work. I have brought in my harvest and the grain is good. Yet I stand with far too few to buy my bread. Those who did are pleased they came and may come again, so for now I am satisfied that I have done enough. I have done enough for now.

6. OK, I am not perfect but I can aim for excellence and that is always better than perfection anyway.

7. I listen to my own criticism, not that of others. My opinion of myself is always constructive, positive and filled with the compassion I deserve.

8. When I do my best at this moment, no matter my faults, I am content that this is enough, for now.

9. I count the strength which is within me to carry on. I have too much to lose, too much of what I am that I have worked and fought hard for, to have it lost. This is where I begin to work and work again, and again and again.

10. When I am with others I can and do feel positive. But when alone with my conscience and inner self to guide me, I think that I would not trade places with anyone, anytime, anyhow.

11. I accept and love myself for who I am, now and forever.

12. I fail, I fail, and I fail again. Here I stand ready to do the impossible, surrounded by my failures. I shall succeed because of my failures and what they have taught me and not in spite of them.

Being Comfortable with Myself

I mentioned vulnerability before but there is more to understand about this state of being and I think it is about being comfortable with ourselves. Our faults and failures are not only acceptable but welcomed when we are comfortable with them.

What did you just say Glenn? Should we welcome our failures? My answer is yes.

I recall a moment of fun I had in a hardware store. I was looking for help with a leaking tap handle in my shower, and my vulnerability was available for strangers to see. The incident went something like this; I saw no-one around and had spent hours in the hardware store searching for the right bits and eventually a young woman came up and asked what I needed. I told her about my leaking tap handle and she immediately looked like she knew what was happening. She said, "I needed a small tool." I felt sure she was joking and I thought I noticed a smirk form across her lips. I replied, "Yes, I did have a small tool already and I offered to show her if it helped in discovery of the right solution." She accepted my inuendo and laughed at the recognition of this double meaning. I added, "You might need a magnifying glass to see it?" To which she guffawed and everyone passing looked in our direction while I continued. She just smiled and proceeded to show me the small tools that would separate the tap from the wall for me and started to walk away. I said, "You probably think I know how to use this, but I don't, can you explain it to me please?" I could almost hear voices in my head saying, "Come on Glenn, you mean you have never changed a tap washer before?" I felt very self-conscience at this point and I said, "I literally have no idea about plumbing and how to fix this kind of stuff." The young woman was very patient with me and added, "You know most men would just take the tool and figure it out by themselves before admitting that I know more than they do about hardware."

I must admit I did feel a little inadequate at the time, and realised that asking for help can be a difficult thing for many people.

Asking for help seems to be a very, difficult thing for some when life presents situations that are life changing and we are exposed with more at stake than some plumbing expertise. I then thought about times when I had to admit huge failures at work, or when I had to accept that I had not lived up to my own expectations of myself. There have certainly been times when my pride has gotten in the way of challenging myself or making a dignified apology or just accepting painful realities about my personal shortcomings. Such personal inadequacies can be painful realisations and it is common for us to avoid such confrontations altogether, rather than face the shame or embarrassment that accompanies such situations.

The good news is I managed to fix my shower, by following the young woman's instructions, with much fumbling, sweating and cursing. I later had a laugh at my lack of handyman skills and relayed it to my good friends at our next BBQ.

I like to think I am comfortable with revealing weaknesses or even failures, but honestly, it can be confronting especially with the big things in life, such as relationship breakups and being fired from a good job, or being embarrassed in public. Such vulnerability can be difficult to accept.

My point here is, that I was comfortable with not only sharing the story but also the banter that made the telling of the story so much fun.

I guess our shared experiences and ongoing support for one another means we are free to talk about almost anything, knowing no one is on guard or likely to be offended and our acceptance of each other as friends is unconditional. In a word I feel very comfortable with my friends and freely express myself as do they.

This I feel is about self-confidence and can be achieved when we are comfortable with ourselves and feeling positive.

This is also the feeling I hope to express as being independent and capable in a demanding world.

CHAPTER 5

BECOMING MORE INDEPENDENT

Independence: that state of being able to work on our own, relying on no one else.

This can be a liberating and highly successful lifestyle. It can also be lonely and a bit frightening, when it is just us against the world. However, the freedom that independence brings is what drives us to remain in this state. Well, until we crave the connection and commitment of others. But being independent does not mean we are alone. Similarly, being in a committed relationship does not mean we are dependent in a negative sense.

Certainly, a move away from being reliant on others for our very existence is a good thing and this is what I refer to as becoming more independent.

A balance, of being self–sufficient and yet remaining connected means that we are not separated from our community or our family and friends, and we enjoy our own individuality.

Some refer to this as being "inter-dependent" and this could be a more positive construct to consider.

"When you wake up in the morning, Pooh" said Piglet at last, "what's the first thing you say to yourself?" "What's for breakfast" said Pooh. "What do you say, Piglet?" "I say, I wonder what's going to happen that is exciting today?" said Piglet. Pooh nodded thoughtfully. "It's the same thing." Said Pooh." AA Milne. R#06.

I believe it is highly motivating to emulate Piglet and say to myself, *"I wonder what's going to happen that is exciting today?"*

The ability to feel the rush of trepidation as excitement and not as fear is liberating to say the least and a great step towards knowing that my actions are the ones that will build my ability to stand on my own actions, that will build my own independence as a person in my own right and to not be reliant on others.

Again, the balance to this idea is naturally that there will be times when it is proper and appropriate to act within a team and for and on behalf of others and to receive generosity and kindness from others.

This next set of affirmations deal with the importance of knowing when we must stand alone and that we are capable and responsible for what we do and how we behave as individuals.

These affirmations I have prepared relate specifically to becoming independent and I am trying to offer some support and guidance for becoming more adult perhaps, but also more outwardly looking to recognise what it is that motivates our process of learning and standing tall as an individual. In this way I am more independent. More independent and able to face the day with whatever exciting expectations I have.

Is Being Independent, Being Selfish?

It is interesting to note that when we are practiced at being independent and capable, we can better act as part of a team and or as a parent or in a leadership role, whenever this is called upon for us to do.

I see this as a progression towards being a key part of a community, a family and the world at large.

This celebration of being part of something larger than ourselves, I will explore in Chapter #6 Gratitude.

For now, these next affirmations offer some assistance and support to the process of becoming independent:

1. I accept that, right now I need help and I am grateful, but sometime very soon I will be able to make my own way in this world.

2. I accept and love myself for who I am, now and forever. I feel capable, confident and ready.

3. I am thankful for everything I hold precious that I have received. Today I am taking charge of myself for a better tomorrow.

4. Yesterday you held me close and I felt loved. Today because you cared, I am strong enough to return that love you so freely gave.

5. One step, two step, three steps done, four steps, five steps, here I come.

6. I hear my breath, I hear my heartbeat, and now I am here and ready for my voice to be heard by you and all the world.

7. Together we are stronger, but dependency may bring weakness, so which is it? I chose to start with being capable and bring that to share with others.

8. I have stopped searching for positivity for the sake of keeping myself and others motivated. My happiness comes from the genuine joy in recognising every step I take towards my hopes, my dreams and goals are working for me.

9. I have defined my success and I am following this every day. This will bring the future I seek.

10. I do not hunger for the approval of others. My path is for me alone. We can rejoice in our progress along the way or whenever we choose to connect our paths. Right now, I continue on the path that is mine.

11. I am letting go of my reliance on my old comfortable habits and replacing them. I am taking those solid bricks in the wall that block me and I am changing them for windows and doors that allow me to see through that wall and past it. I now see clearly where I want to be.

12. I am able to say thank you to others who care for me, without a feeling of obligation. I choose to do what I need to do for myself and this feels right for me to grow.

GRATITUDE.

CHAPTER 6

LIVING IN A STATE OF GRATITUDE

People say to me that being grateful for the things they have or have been given, or have experienced, brings them more happiness than anything else in their life.

It certainly does bring great joy, when this happens. I also witness an almost doubling of the joy that is shared in giving thanks for kind deeds and welcomed support and so in this way expressing gratitude has a multiplying effect that I also refer to as *abundance*. Feel welcome to check out what I have to say about abundance in my earlier book *"Yes. I Can Handle Three Things For Now"*.

These and other benefits of expressing gratitude come from reflective thinking of all those things we sometimes take for granted such as; people being kind, clean running water straight to our kitchen or bathroom taps, clean fresh air which is a courtesy from the trees and plants that grow on our planet earth, and so many other natural wonders, just to name a few.

I also want to give thanks to all who love and express care and regard for me, every wish for my comfort and happiness is a joy forever.

Sadly, I note also that some people are adverse to accepting help when offered and actually regard this act as creating an obligation to reciprocate or even being weak, or in some way cheating because they are not acting independently or do not see themselves as having enough worthiness to be deserving of such gifts!

Certainly, being independently strong and capable is a virtuous quality, but limiting support offered to us from others can cause us to become reclusive and bitter. Indeed, by excluding support or gifts from others can be disrespectful of those who are offering so generously.

When separating ourselves from the very community that we also may be proud to contribute to, and to support, is not helpful. My previous chapter on *independence* covers some of that, but I feel it is beneficial that once achieving a state of independence to then move forward towards gratitude, is a completion of that inter-dependence that I mentioned earlier.

I advocate that, by acting together, we are more capable than acting alone. I feel that just the thought of being part of a community, gives us the opportunity to interact with others, grow in a balanced perspective of the world around us and we can achieve whatever we want whilst being supported in our efforts.

The peace we seek is not attached to the things and accomplishments we chase with furious desire but within the methods we use to achieve our hopes, dreams and goals. Within us is our calm, our courage and our strength. This has always been with us, deep within our own hearts. *(My own words, but taught to me through meditation R#07)*

So often I hear people say that the adversity they have experienced has made them stronger than what they were prior to these harrowing experiences. I seriously doubt this is the case. Because, if they were in some way deficient before the experience then they could not have possibly been successful in these dealings.

For me such strength and personal conviction to deal with adversity lies within us all and has been there all the time. I do instead recognise that such adversity will awaken our inner capability and facilitate it by the acquisition of skills previously not held. But our pre-existing strength is always there and can be relied upon to be present when we do reach for it in those times of need.

Often, we need to remember this, rather than expect to be overwhelmed because we are having a new experience.

When I reflect on the concept of community, that I share with so many, it appears to me to be a friendly, welcoming and supportive place. A place where I live, grow and prosper to share my own commonwealth. It is a place where others are also growing and developing skills and discovering capabilities through both adversity and the simple act of living. This is also a place where, generosity abounds, experiences are shared and where love grows. For this I feel truly grateful.

I feel that I can elicit this feeling of gratitude, and give my thanks, through the following affirmations:

1. I have many reasons to be happy and peaceful. I am grateful for them all.

2. I accept that life is all at once; good, bad and indifferent and I choose to celebrate that which brings joy and love to all.

3. I have many things to do, and I shall prepare myself for these by taking time now to be thankful for that which has been given to me to make these happen.

4. Those deep, deep valleys are now far below me as I stand here on my mountain peak contemplating my next deep dive and yet another climb, before I can rest again.

5. I have truly found peace within my own heart, because of the positive values I have lived.

6. I see it beautifully framed by these squared timbers. There it is, just outside my window, I see the sky, the earth, its beauty and its strength and I am again in love with this gift of place that the world has offered to me every moment of my existence.

How Broad is Your Wingspan?

How often have you watched and marveled at a soaring eagle or a large sea bird riding the thermals way above us here on the ground and then watched her gently touch down on her nest of young chicks?

And then have you imagined how they do that?

It is doubly fascinating to see how this majestic creature of the sky, comforts and protects her young in a manner that is perfect for them. Her wingspan covers all her chicks, not just one or two and it is strong enough and comforting enough to give them the courage to do the same, generation after generation.

There is something special about that wingspan and it reaches its correct proportion for each stage of its life. First it is strong enough to take that first flight, then to support itself in growth to full adulthood and then in seeking a mate. Finally, it provides a full shelter to its own young.

Our own wingspan is not just the physical distance from fingertip to fingertip but if I speak metaphorically, it is how far we reach beyond our own selves and touch the hearts and minds of others.

For many this wingspan will embrace the one that we love, or even further to protect and love for our families, both large and small. Family of course represents not only those connected through blood and law, but includes those friends we meet .... the ones who then *become* our family.

Is it possible for each of us to make a contribution to that larger community and influence or impact in a positive way, perfect strangers, people we work with and even those we compete with? Could this be our potential wingspan?

At times our wingspan may reach those we may never meet in person. By our actions we can make their lives a little richer than it would otherwise be without us in the world. Many celebrities, those in public office, teachers and professionals, and volunteers active in our communities certainly achieve this. I am grateful to them all. Some are still making an impact that will change the way others think and act and then inspire and give warmth and comfort to thousands in the future. I personally welcome all positive influences in my life and this includes those non-celebrities as well!

I also reflect on what I can do myself, and hope that in some way I too can add to and build on this great body of work that is our society. It may be that we are meant as a species to be and live with others, even though at times we can feel suffocated.

Eventually, we all have the potential to reach out and offer a welcoming wingspan to guide and touch others and to feel the warmth and support from others when our own hearts need it.

I do subscribe to the axiom, *"It takes a village,"* to live, love and build a legacy for future generations.

Here are some affirmations that may fit this theme of community and being grateful for others as well as the peace I find when all is said and done:

7. I surround myself with people who are kind, welcoming and inclusive. They are my constant inspiration and my greatest companions.

8. My friends and family support me to achieve my goals and I am thankful for all they do for me.

9. Happiness is something that just happens, usually when I least expect it or when I stop searching for it. I truly love how it sneaks up on me.

10. It is not enough that I seek success, I now realise that I am able to seek, find and hold my success through exploring what I want, how I express it and why I want it. Suddenly, my success seems highly achievable.

11. I know not what is before me. I only know that I have faced such trials before and am confident they can and will be overcome. For this I am eternally grateful.

12. There was a time when I could not imagine the wealth and happiness I now feel. I am truly thankful for all that has happened from that time until now.

Our values must be;
defined,
challenged, and
lived.
Choose one and apply .....
I choose KINDNESS ;)
Glenn ☺

ACKNOWLEDGEMENTS:

To all those listed and to so many others, with whom I consult daily and who continue to inspire, support and critique my constant ramblings. May we never stop sharing the big ideas!

Lena Agha
Alan Bruce
Carli Desborough-Clark
Kirsty Hilton
Donna Redman
Leisa Trigg-Saleh

REFERENCES:

R#01: Glenn Cossar, *Yes. I Can Handle Three Things For Now*, (Balboa Press, 2017) P340

R#02: Dr Carmen Harra, https://www.huffingtonpost.com/dr-carmen-harra/affirmations_b_3527028.html

R#03: Kate James, *Build Resilience& Free Yourself From Fear*, (Affirm Press, 2018) P83

R#04: Frank Herbert, *Dune*, (Victor Gallance LTD, 1966, New English Library NEL, 1968) P 19

R#05: Jane Goodall, https://www.goodreads.com/author/quotes/18163.Jane_Goodall

R#06: A A Milne, *Winnie-the-Pooh*, (Methuen Children's Books, 1926) P156

R#07: Mahasiddha Kadampa Meditation Centre Sydney http://meditateinsydney.org

One final affirmation from me ……… please use the next page to write your own.

I am now and always shall be at peace with myself.
This gives me the strength
to see the joy and love in others.
This carries me forward
without doubt, without fear, and I am truly happy.

Glenn ☺

NOTES: MY OWN AFFIRMATIONS.

NOTES: MY OWN AFFIRMATIONS.

NOTES: MY OWN AFFIRMATIONS.

NOTES: MY OWN AFFIRMATIONS.

Printed in the United States
By Bookmasters